IMAGES
of America

COLTON

Formerly the Colton Public Library, this Classical Revival–style building at 380 North La Cadena Drive is now the home of the Colton Area Museum. Construction of the building was funded by a grant from the Andrew Carnegie Foundation. The building opened in 1908 and served as the public library until 1983, when the library moved to a new building on Ninth and D Streets. After extensive renovation and retrofitting, the building reopened in December 1991 as the Colton Area Museum. (Photo by Pat and Bernie Skehan, courtesy of CAM.)

IMAGES
of America

COLTON

Larry Sheffield

ARCADIA
PUBLISHING

Copyright © 2004 by Larry Sheffield
ISBN 978-1-5316-1532-1

Published by Arcadia Publishing
Charleston, South Carolina

Library of Congress Catalog Card Number: 2004104889

For all general information contact Arcadia Publishing at:
Telephone 843-853-2070
Fax 843-853-0044
E-mail sales@arcadiapublishing.com
For customer service and orders:
Toll-Free 1-888-313-2665

Visit us on the Internet at www.arcadiapublishing.com

Designed by Riverside Graphics in 1999, Colton's official city logo features the Colton Carnegie Building, now the home of the Colton Area Museum, and is meant to express a new era in Colton's history. (Courtesy of the City of Colton.)

CONTENTS

Acknowledgments   6

Introduction   7

1.   Forerunners   9

2.   Founding, 1874–1899   27

3.   Hometown, U.S.A., 1900–1949   57

4.   Suburban Community, 1950–Present   105

ACKNOWLEDGMENTS

Several organizations and individuals contributed to this project. The Colton Area Museum, Pam Gregory, secretary/manager of the Colton Chamber of Commerce, and Johnnie Ralphs, librarian of the Pfau Library at the California State University, allowed me to scan images from their photo archives. Don Hines, a Colton native, generously shared his firsthand knowledge of the city with me and read many of the captions. Bobby Vasquez, also a Colton native, introduced me to the photo collection at Cal State and guided me through the history of South Colton. Janet Cosgrove, vice president of the Colton Area Museum Association, read all the captions and offered many helpful suggestions. John Adams and Richard McInnif of the Rialto Historical Society gave me a very helpful tutorial in scanning. Angel Cisneros, network technician for the City of Colton, and Pat Barlow, Colton Area Museum docent, provided invaluable technical assistance. And finally, the editorial staff at Arcadia Publishing provided support and encouragement throughout the project. To all, I give my heartfelt thanks.

Throughout the text, certain images are followed with these photo credits: *Century Annals of San Bernardino County* by Luther A. Ingersoll, 1904 (CASBC); the California Room, San Bernardino Public Library (CRSBPL); the Colton Area Museum (CAM).

INTRODUCTION

Since its founding 129 years ago, Colton has grown from a township of approximately 1 square mile to a city of nearly 18 square miles. This growth has come through the annexation of neighboring areas, many of which have their own unique histories predating the founding of Colton proper. With the annexation of these areas, Colton has broadened the scope of its history, making it one of the most historic cities in the San Bernardino Valley.

The first people to inhabit what is today Colton were Native Americans—Gabrielino and Serrano—who lived in villages near the Santa Ana River and in Reche Canyon. Spanish explorers in search of an overland route from Mexico to Monterey passed through or near Colton in the 1770s. Franciscan missionaries from Mission San Gabriel established a presence in the Colton area in the early 1880s. The Rancho period saw the creation of the San Bernardino and Jurupa Ranchos, portions of which are now within the boundaries of Colton. Immigrants from New Mexico arrived in the San Bernardino Valley via the Old Spanish Trail in the 1840s and founded Agua Mansa, now a part of Colton, and the Mormon colonization of San Bernardino in 1851 brought English and American settlers to what is today Colton.

The Southern Pacific Railroad Company founded the town site of Colton in 1875, naming it after David Douty Colton, vice president of the railroad company at the time. Within a few months, the company built water towers and a train station, and the first residents of the town site arrived. Among these first residents were transplants from Tennessee, Alabama, Massachusetts, Illinois, Pennsylvania, and Kansas, and they were soon joined by descendants of the New Mexican founders of Agua Mansa, who moved into the southern section of the town site from the neighboring area of San Salvador.

In 1883, the California Southern Railroad extended its line from San Diego through Colton to San Bernardino, making Colton the transportation hub of the San Bernardino Valley. By 1887, Colton's population had grown to slightly more than 1,000 people, and in April of that year the town incorporated as a city of the sixth class.

Because of its location at the junction of two transcontinental railways, Colton became the citrus processing and shipping center of the San Bernardino Valley and one of the largest citrus shipping points in the state. The city's economic base underwent significant expansion in 1891, when the California Portland Cement Company began mining limestone on Slover Mountain, and again in 1907, when the Pacific Fruit Express opened its rail car pre-cooling plant in Colton.

Throughout the first half of the 20th century, Colton had the appearance of "Hometown U.S.A.," a nearly self-contained and ethnically divided community built around a downtown area comprising professional offices, shops, department stores, movie theaters, restaurants, and soda fountains.

7

Colton underwent significant changes during the 1950s and 1960s. The city became more ethnically integrated during the post–World War II years. Interstate 10 replaced J Street, the city's first commercial district, and annexations expanded the city's boundaries and history. New shopping centers opened, and most of the buildings making up the downtown section were demolished as part of various redevelopment projects. Today, Colton is a diverse suburban city, but its proximity to freeways and railroads still make it the transportation hub of the San Bernardino Valley.

Don Earp, left, a cousin of Wyatt Earp, and Larry Fisher linked the past with the present at the Earp exhibit in the Colton Area Museum during a museum open house in 2002. (Photo by Larry Sheffield.)

This photo captures the spirit of Colton as "Hub City." The view looks to the south, where the Union Pacific and Burlington Northern & Santa Fe tracks cross under Interstate 10. (Courtesy of the Colton Chamber of Commerce.)

One

FORERUNNERS

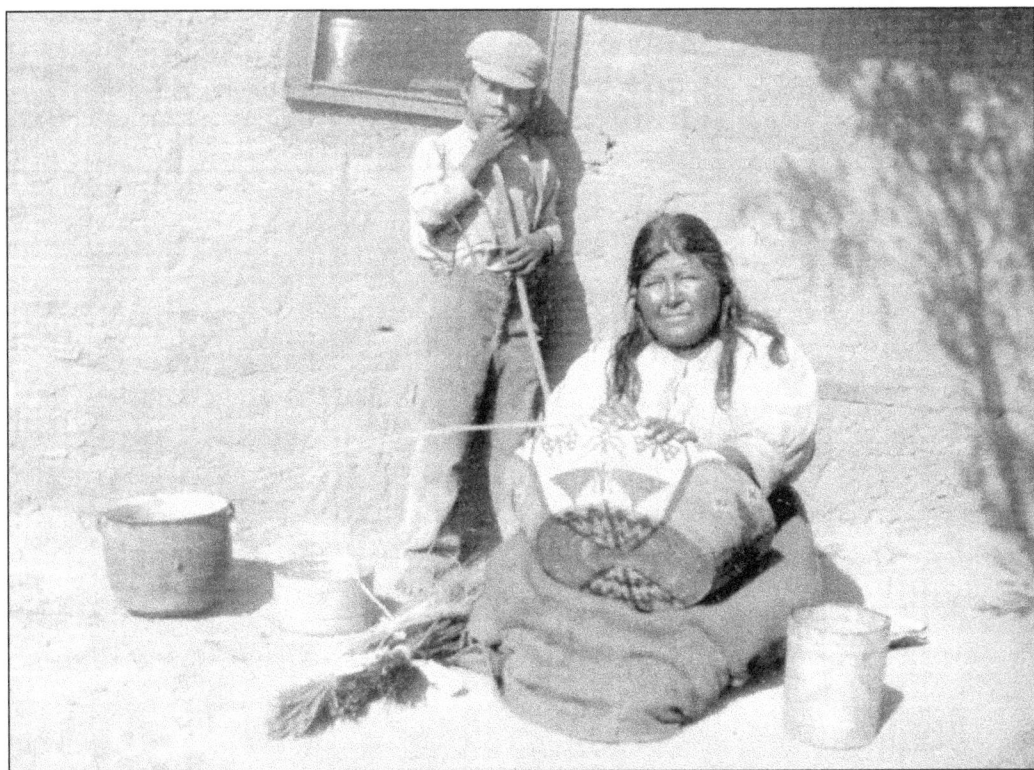

The first people to live in what is today Colton were Gabrielino and Serrano Indians. The Serrano had villages in the vicinity of Hunt's Lane, immediately north of Interstate 10, and in Reche Canyon. Shown in this c. 1900 photograph is Louisa Pino, a Serrano woman, making a tule basket. (Courtesy of Pauline Murillo.)

9

Don Antonio Lugo, owner of the Rancho San Antonio (near present-day Compton) and the Rancho Santa Ana del Chino, used his influence with California governor Juan Alvarado to help his sons, Carmen del Lugo, Vicente Lugo, and Maria Lugo, and his nephew, Diego Sepulveda, acquire a grant to the Rancho San Bernardino in 1842. (Courtesy of CAM.)

Much of present-day Colton was once part of the Rancho San Bernardino and the Rancho Jurupa. (Courtesy of CRSBPL.)

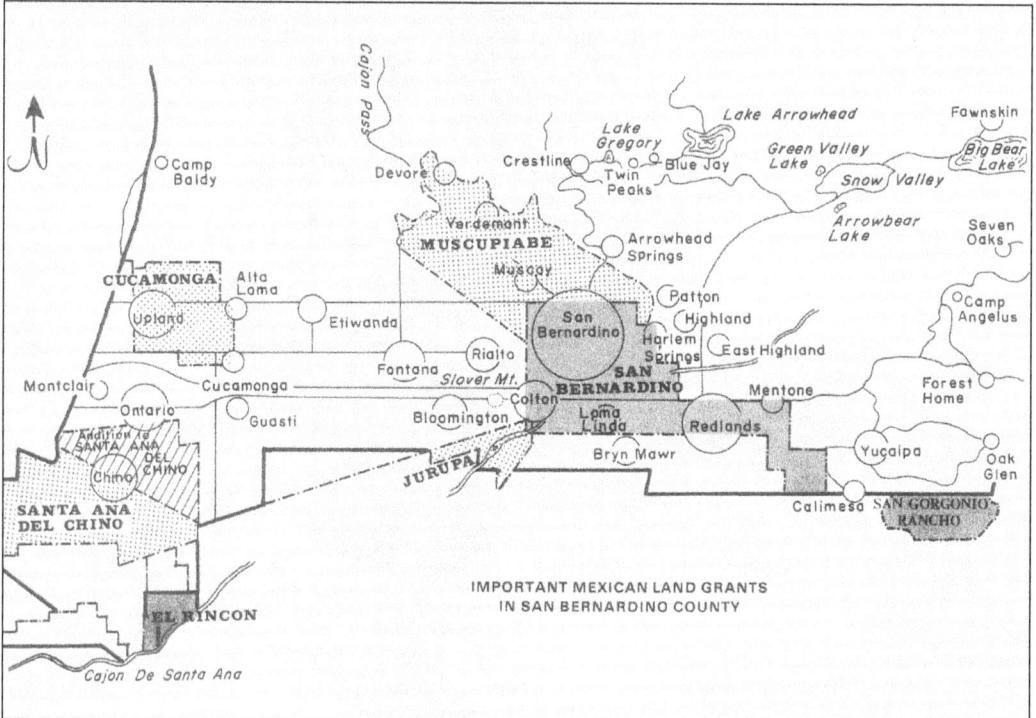

IMPORTANT MEXICAN LAND GRANTS
IN SAN BERNARDINO COUNTY

Livestock grazing on the Rancho San Bernardino were easy prey for cattle rustlers and horse thieves. One of the most troublesome marauders was the Ute Indian chief Wakara, shown here (left) with his brother Arapene. Wakara led periodic raids on the Lugo's livestock, especially horses and mules. In an attempt to protect their herds, the Lugos made a deal with Lorenzo Trujillo, a visitor from Abiquiu, New Mexico, to provide free land on the Rancho San Bernardino to settlers from Abiquiu who were willing to fend off Native-American raiders. Trujillo subsequently recruited several Abiqueno families who settled on a section of the rancho known as Politana, named after one of its residents, Hipolitio Espinosa. These pioneer families eventually founded Agua Mansa, now a part of Colton, and their descendents became the nucleus of Colton's present-day Latino population. (Drawing by Frederick Piercy, a contemporary of Wakara and Arapene.)

San Bernardino historian Nick Cataldo gives perspective to this photograph of an empty field that was once the location of Politana. The building behind Nick is the Prophet Saint Elias Greek Orthodox Church atop Bunker Hill along Colton Avenue. (Courtesy of Nick Cataldo.)

Between 1844 and 1845, following a dispute with the Lugos, the Abiqueno settlers at Politana accepted an offer from Juan Bandini (shown here) of free land on a section of his Rancho Jurupa, about five miles to the southwest, on the Santa Ana River. In return they agreed to protect his livestock. The section became known as the Bandini Donation. There, the settlers founded two communities, La Placita on the south side of the river, and Agua Mansa (Gentle Waters) on the north side of the river. Together, the two communities became known as San Salvador. Both communites were destroyed by a flood in January 1862. After the flood, several Agua Mansans moved to higher ground in the vicinity of today's Agua Mansa Road and Rancho Avenue, where they established a new settlement. This settlement also became known as San Salvador. Agua Mansa and the second settlement of San Salvador are now part of Colton. (Courtesy of CASBC.)

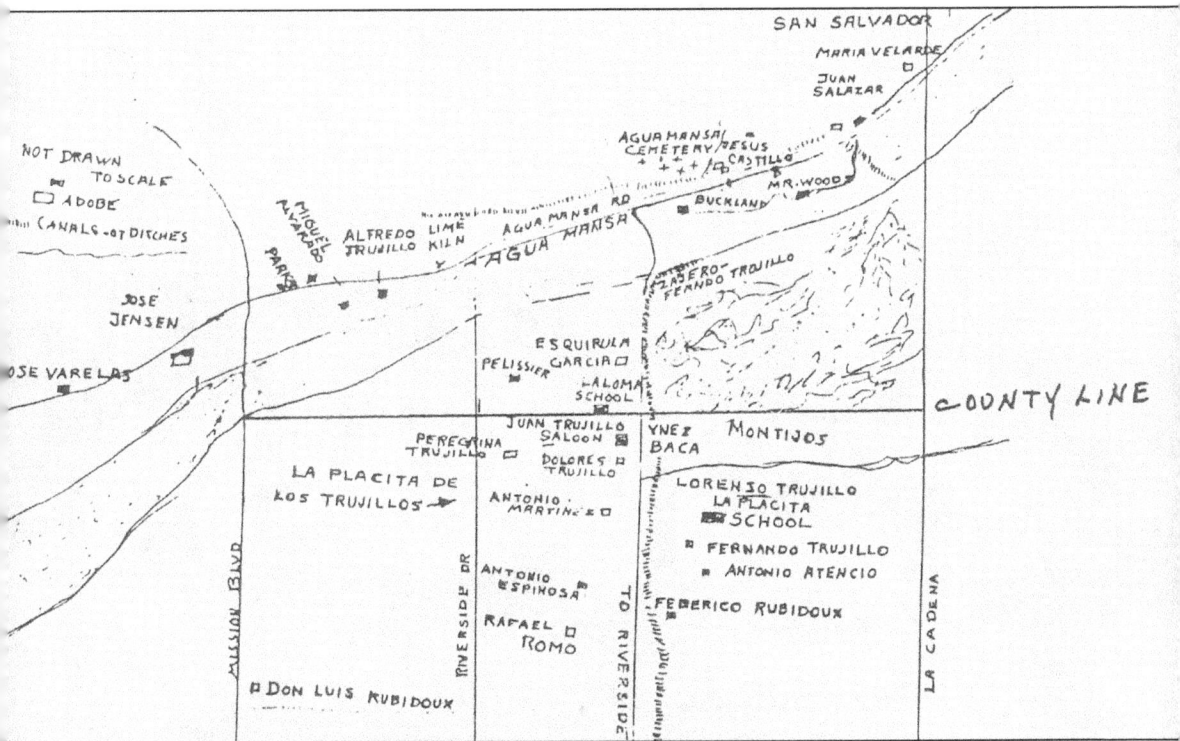

This map, drawn from memory by Salvador Alvarado in 1976, shows the approximate layout of La Placita and Agua Mansa along the Santa Ana River. The river runs diagonally between the two communities. Agua Mansa is shown on the northerly, or upper, bank and La Placita on the southern bank. (Map courtesy of *The Agua Mansa History Trail* by R. Bruce Harley, 1996.)

Shown here is the second San Salvador Church, which was built in Agua Mansa in 1853 after the first San Salvador Church, built in La Placita in 1852, sank in quicksand. The Agua Mansa chapel was located just east of the Agua Mansa Cemetery and remained in use until about 1878. According to historian R. Bruce Harley, area residents subsequently attended services in San Bernardino until 1912, when a third San Salvador Church was built on K Street in Colton. The present chapel on K and Seventh Streets is the fourth San Salvador Church. (Courtesy of CASBC.)

Miguel Bustamente, a native of Sonora, Mexico, who settled in Agua Mansa in 1852, laid the shake roof of the chapel at Agua Mansa. He also served as the first official postmaster of Agua Mansa and served on the San Salvador school board. (Courtesy of CASBC.)

The Agua Mansa Museum and caretaker quarters, now located at the Agua Mansa Cemetery, is a replica of the original Agua Mansa chapel. The replica was dedicated in June 1978. (Photo by Larry Sheffield.)

This undated photo shows the Agua Mansa Cemetery before fires and vandals destroyed the wooden crosses. The first recorded burial in the cemetery took place in 1854 and the last in 1963. Among the Agua Mansa pioneers buried here are Lorenzo Trujillo and Cornelius and Mercedes (Alvarado) Jensen. The cemetery is now under the jurisdiction of the San Bernardino County Museum. (Courtesy of CRSBPL.)

A sea captain from the Frisian island of Sylt off the coast of Denmark, Cornelius Jensen settled in Agua Mansa in about 1854 and became a prominent businessman and community leader. Shortly after moving to Agua Mansa, he married Mercedes Alvarado and established a home next to the Agua Mansa chapel. The home also served as a general store, post office, and stage stop. In the ensuing years, Jensen developed extensive business interests and served four terms as chairman of the San Bernardino County Board of Supervisors. In 1870, the Jensens moved to a ranch in what is today Rubidoux. Their Rubidoux home and ranch are now registered state historic landmarks. (Courtesy of CASBC.)

Mercedes Alvarado Jensen, shown here, was a daughter of Francisco and Juana Maria (Avila) Alvarado. Historian R. Bruce Harley has pointed out that two other Alvarado daughters also married men who became prominent in Agua Mansa and San Bernardino County history. Refugio Alvarado married Peter Peters, and Dolores Alvarado married Fenton Slaughter. Like his brother-in-law, Cornelius Jensen, Slaughter served on the San Bernardino County Board of Supervisors. (Courtesy of CASBC.)

The home of Peter and Refugio (Alvarado) Peters is still standing on the southwest corner of Rancho Avenue and Agua Mansa Drive. This area became the location of the new community of San Salvador after the flood of 1862 destroyed Agua Mansa. Peter Peters was a native of the island of Sylt near Denmark, and a cousin of Cornelius Jensen. He served on the San Salvador school board and as a trustee of the Agua Mansa cemetery. Peter and Refugio later moved to a home in South Colton. (Courtesy of CAM.)

When the first San Salvador School at Agua Mansa was destroyed by the devastating flood of 1862, the Agua Mansans established a second San Salvador School in a one-room adobe house near the northeast corner of today's Agua Mansa Road and Rancho Avenue. This second school, shown here, remained in use as a school until the late 1800s, when a new school building, the third San Salvador School, was constructed nearby. (Courtesy of CAM.)

Ellison Robbins, a native of New York and graduate of Hamilton College, taught in the second San Salvador School from 1863 to 1864. When he died in 1864, his widow, Eliza, moved into the school and taught his classes until the end of the term. She later married Myron Crafts, after whom Crafton, California, is named. (Courtesy of *Pioneer Days in the San Bernardino Valley* by Mrs. E.P.R. Crafts, 1906.)

19

Tom Quiroz, head custodian at the present San Salvador School, stands on the site of the second San Salvador School. The present San Salvador School is located to his right. (Photo by Larry Sheffield.)

Today, Agua Mansa is undergoing industrial development. Shown here is the Colton/San Bernardino Rapid Infiltration and Extraction Facility (sewage treatment) on Agua Mansa Road, near the cemetery. (Photo by Larry Sheffield.)

James M. and Lucinda Coburn, shown here on the front porch of their home on present-day Coburn Avenue, settled on the property in 1854 and established a farm. The area later became known as Bethune, the name of a Southern Pacific Motor Road station located on the corner of Coburn and Colton Avenues. The City of Colton annexed Bethune in 1940. (Courtesy of Carlos Bastida.)

This view of the Coburn house today is from Colton Avenue looking north and shows the south side of the house. (Photo by Larry Sheffield, courtesy of Carlos Bastida.)

George and Ellen (Tolputt) Cooley, English converts to Mormonism, met and married on board the ship *Camillus* while emigrating to the United States in 1853. After a brief sojourn in Salt Lake City, they joined a party of emigrants, which included Ambrose Hunt and family, headed for San Bernardino. Upon arriving in San Bernardino in 1857, the Cooley and Hunt families camped near the former Indian village of Jumuba on today's Hunt's Lane. Both families established ranches in the area. The Cooleys established their ranch on approximately 400 acres of land in the vicinity of today's Mt. Vernon Avenue, south of the Santa Ana River. The City of Colton annexed the Cooley Ranch area in the 1960s. The former ranch is now a commercial and industrial center. (Courtesy of *The Story of Colton* by Elma Maltsberger, 1974.)

This *c.* 1885 photograph shows the Cooley Ranch and the Cooleys' two-story house. (Courtesy of *The Story of Colton* by Elma Maltsberger, 1974.)

Cooley House was decorated in the Victorian style popular at the time. The ceilings in the parlor, shown here, and in the study and kitchen, featured hand-painted designs. George Cooley hired artists for the Pullman Company to do the ceiling decorations during a strike in 1894. In accordance with Pullman practices, the artists painted the designs on strips of canvas, which they then glued to the ceilings in panels. (Courtesy of CAM.)

Shown here are the nine Cooley sons. Seated, from left to right, are John (Jack), George M., and Edward (Ted). Standing, from left to right, are Norman, William, Charles, Frank, Fred, and Scott. (Courtesy of CAM.)

23

As late as 1973, cattle could still be seen grazing in the former Cooley Ranch pasture. (Courtesy of CRSBPL.)

Today, Ashley Furniture Company is located on the former Cooley Ranch pasture. (Photo by Larry Sheffield.)

24

The House Grain Company on Hunt's Lane just south of Interstate 10 is located on a historically significant site. Once well watered by three springs and lush with greenery, the area was originally the site of the village of Jumuba, inhabited by Gabrielino, and later Serrano Indians. Jedediah Smith, the first American to enter California by land, camped here in January 1827. The land was later granted to the Lugos as part of the Rancho San Bernardino. From 1856 to 1857, Jerome Benson established a farm and Fort Benson here. Ambrose Hunt, after whom Hunt's Lane is named, acquired Benson's farm and built a family home in the area. Bulldozers leveled the area when the freeway was built in the 1950s. A plaque mounted on the pedestal in front of the House Grain Company now commemorates the site. (Photo by Larry Sheffield.)

Fort Benson, once located in the vicinity of the House Grain Company, was a flash point in the dissension between Mormons and non-Mormons in the Mormon colony of San Bernardino. In 1857, shortly after Jerome Benson, a former Mormon, settled on the property, church authorities in San Bernardino, claiming the land belonged to them, initiated eviction proceedings. In defiance, Benson and other non-Mormons, calling themselves "Independents," fortified Benson's barn by installing a small cannon they brought from San Bernardino in the middle window. As it turned out, the Mormons evacuated San Bernardino later that year, and Benson acquired legal title to the property. The cannon is now mounted in front of the Native Sons of the Golden West headquarters in San Bernardino. (Courtesy of CASBC.)

Two

FOUNDING

1874–1899

In this 1877 photo, the locomotive *General Grant* crosses the Santa Ana River on its way to the Southern Pacific depot in Colton. (Courtesy of CAM.)

In 1874, William A. Conn, a San Bernardino businessman and state legislator, sold a 2,000-acre section of the former Rancho San Bernardino to William H. Mintzer, P.A. Raynor, Ambrose Hunt, and James C. Peacock, M.D., known collectively as the Slover Mountain Colony Association. On April 17, 1875, the colony association, which now included two new members, William Riley Fox, M.D., and Rev. James C. Cameron, in turn sold 604 acres of the section to the Western Development Company, the construction arm of the Southern Pacific Railroad, for use as a town site. Officials of the Southern Pacific Company named the new town site Colton after David Douty Colton, vice president of the Southern Pacific Railroad at the time. (Courtesy of CASBC.)

Born in Monson, Maine in 1831, David D. Colton came to California in 1850 to mine for gold. He eventually settled in San Francisco, where he invested in mining ventures and was active in state politics. In 1874, he became an associate of Collis P. Huntington, Leland Stanford, Charles Crocker, and Mark Hopkins, owners of the Central and Southern Pacific Railroad companies, and became vice president of the Southern Pacific Railroad in 1875. He died three years later of injuries he received when a horse he was riding fell on him. He was buried at Mountain View Cemetery in Oakland, California. His home on Nob Hill in San Francisco is now the Huntington Children's Park. (California State Library.)

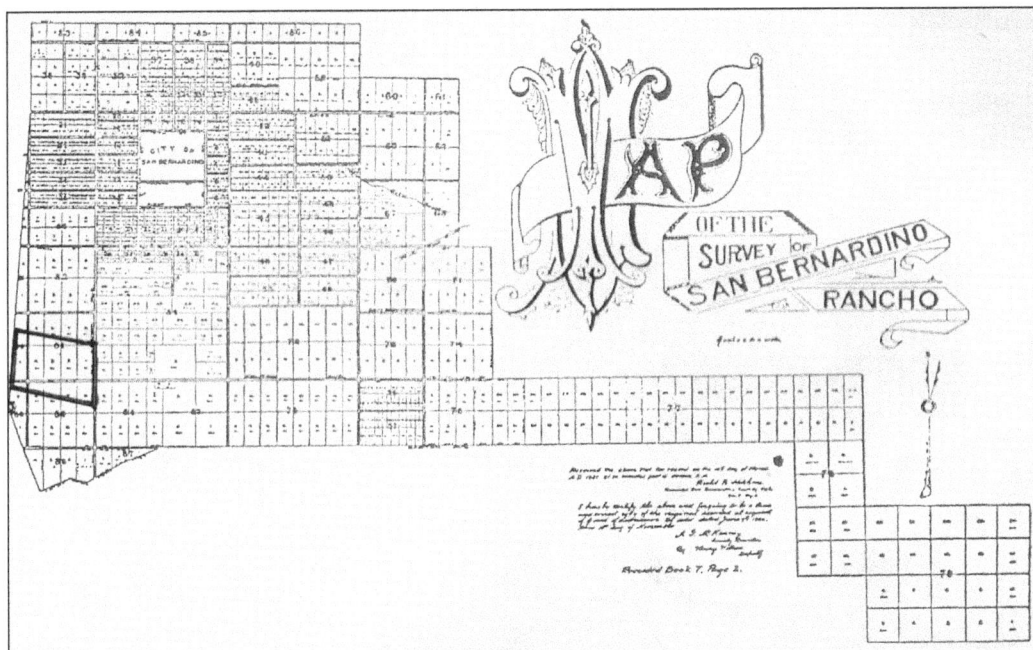

The boxed area shows the location of the original town site of Colton on Fred Perris's 1857 survey map of the Rancho San Bernardino. The boundaries of the town site, in terms of present-day streets, were Rancho Avenue on the west, E Street on the north, Mount Vernon Avenue on the east, and O Street on the south. (Courtesy of CRSBPL.)

James C. Peacock, M.D., was one of the original members of the Slover Mountain Colony Association. A former county physician and postmaster in San Bernardino, he moved to Colton where he developed the Peacock Block along the east side of Ninth Street between the alley and J Street. The block included lodgings, restaurants, and a clothing store. The area is now part of Interstate 10. (Courtesy of CAM.)

William Riley Fox, M.D., a San Bernardino physician, joined the Slover Mountain Colony Association shortly before it sold the land for the town site of Colton. Dr. Fox built a home and established an orange orchard just outside the original town site. He was one of the founders of the Colton Presbyterian Church and was vice president of the First National Bank of Colton. (Courtesy of CAM.)

Minnie (Benedict) Fox was the wife of William Riley Fox, M.D. (Courtesy of CAM.)

The Reverend James C. Cameron was a missionary in San Bernardino when he joined the Slover Mountain Colony Association. He conducted the first religious service in the new townsite of Colton and was a founder and first pastor of the Colton First Presbyterian Church. He and his wife, Emma, established a home and orange orchard on land adjacent to the Fox home. The Camerons moved to Oakland, California, in 1878. Reverend Cameron died there in 1882. (Courtesy of the First Presbyterian Church of Colton.)

Emma S. Cameron, wife of Reverend Cameron, became the first president of the Presbyterian Women's Home Mission Society shortly after she and her husband moved to Oakland. (Courtesy of the First Presbyterian Church of Colton.)

Built in 1875, the Southern Pacific depot has been remodeled several times over the years. The building still stands at its original location on Ninth Street and is now occupied by the Cal–Wal Gypsum Company. (Courtesy of CAM).

This typical 1870s passenger train is parked along side the Southern Pacific roundhouse in Colton. (Courtesy of CAM.)

Taken in 1875, this photograph shows some of the first residents of Colton. Sitting, from left to right, are Winston House, Jacob Polhemus, Mr. and Mrs. Laird, Henry Gregory, Jim Gibson, William Montgomery Gregory, and M.A. Murphy. Standing, from left to right, are Leroy E. Mosher, John Congrieve, John Butler, Frank Emerson, and Will Polhemus. (Courtesy of CASBC.)

Shortly after completing its depot, the Southern Pacific Railroad built a small park where train passengers could stretch their legs during stops. Railroad Park, as it came to be known, was located between the depot and J Street, and extended from Ninth Street to Eighth Street. The park was landscaped with semitropical plants, had winding pathways, and was bordered by pepper trees. The park was razed in 1954 to make way for Interstate 10. (Courtesy of CAM.)

In the fall of 1876, William M. Godfrey, shown here, and S.M. Franklin founded the *Colton Advocate and Southern California Advertiser*, Colton's first newspaper and the progenitor of today's *Colton Courier*. Godfrey renamed the newspaper the *Semi-Tropic and Southern California Advertiser*. (Courtesy of CASBC.)

Scipio Craig bought the *Semi-Tropic* from William Godfrey in April 1877. In his last issue as owner and editor, Godfrey wrote: "Good-bye Godfrey! Good morning Craig." Craig operated the paper until 1880, when he moved to Redlands, where he founded the *Citrograph*. (Courtesy of CASBC.)

The first schoolhouses in the town site of Colton were located on the north side of I Street just east of the present-day Burlington, Northern & Santa Fe railroad tracks. The school on the right was built in about 1876 and remained in use until the new school on the left was built in 1884. Mrs. David Colton donated the funds for construction of the new school in memory of her late husband. She also donated a bell for the school. This schoolhouse was later sold, and the proceeds of the sale were used to help pay for construction of the first Lincoln School. The fate of the school bell is unknown. (Courtesy of CAM.)

Workers at the Southern Pacific roundhouse kept locomotives in operating condition. (Courtesy of CAM.)

Founded in 1877, the First Presbyterian Church of Colton was the first church established in the town site. The chapel shown here was located on the northeast corner of Eighth and H Streets and served the congregation from 1877 until 1951, when the congregation built a new chapel at 710 West C Street. (Courtesy of the First Presbyterian Church of Colton.)

Colton Marble and Lime Company.

COLTON MARBLE & LIME CO.
MARBLE WORKS

COLTON, CALIFORNIA

MANUFACTURERS OF THE CELEBRATED
DIAMOND & MARBLE LIME
THE STRONGEST AND BEST FINISHING LIME MADE
ON THE PACIFIC COAST, PORTLAND CEMENT GRAND
RAPIDS PLASTER AND LAND PLASTER ALWAYS ON HAND

BUILDING & DIMENSION STONE
CUT, CARVED OR SAWED.
MONUMENTAL & CEMETERY WORK
IN ALL ITS BRANCHES.

The Colton Lime and Marble Company conducted mining operations on Slover Mountain from 1881 until 1892, when the California Portland Cement Company took it over and began its mining operations on the mountain. (Courtesy of CAM.)

37

Pictured here is C.P. Sims's grocery delivery service. (Courtesy of CAM.)

Virgil Earp became a resident of Colton in 1882. His left arm had been permanently disabled by a blast of pellets from an ambusher's shotgun in the bloody aftermath of the shootout near the OK Corral in Tombstone. Nevertheless, he found work in Colton as a special agent for the Southern Pacific Railroad and won election as constable of the Colton Township. When the city was incorporated in 1887, he won election as the first city marshal. He served as city marshal from July 1887 until March 1889, when he resigned. (Courtesy of CAM.)

This house was the Colton home of Virgil and Allie Earp from 1888 until 1891. The house is now a registered city landmark. (Courtesy of CAM.)

VIRGIL EARP FAMILY HOME
COLTON, CALIFORNIA

When Morgan Earp was killed by an assassin's bullet in the aftermath of the shootout in Tombstone, his body, accompanied by his brother Virgil, was transported to Colton for burial. (Courtesy of CAM.)

U. S. DEPUTY MARSHAL
MORGAN S. EARP
BORN 1851
ASSASSINATED
TOMBSTONE ARIZONA
MARCH 18, 1882

Initially buried in the cemetery at the base of Slover Mountain, Morgan Earp's body was later reinterred at Hermosa Cemetery. (Courtesy of CAM.)

Colton's first citrus fair, held in 1886 in the Colton Cannery on Tenth Street between I and J Streets, included this display of citrus products by Dr. William Riley Fox and his brother Abram Stoner Fox. (Courtesy of CAM.)

John W. Davis Sr. was a founder and first president of the First National Bank of Colton. The bank opened for business in 1886 and remained in existence until 1928 when it was acquired by the Bank of America, thus giving Colton's present-day branch of the Bank of America a 118-year tradition of banking in the city. (Courtesy of CASBC.)

Built by John and Martha Davis (not related to John W. Davis Sr.) in 1886, this hotel stood on the northwest corner of Ninth and L Streets. The hotel underwent several name changes. The Davises named it Hotel Davis. When Mrs. Davis sold it following the death of her husband, the new owner renamed it the Marlborough Hotel. By the time this photo was taken in 1894, the hotel had been renamed Hotel Colton. The hotel was demolished in 1921. (Courtesy of CAM.)

Cole and Stetson Livery Stable hired out horses and carriages and operated a passenger and mail stagecoach line between Colton, Needles, Daggett, and Yuma. The stable was located on the southeast corner of Eighth and I Streets in the 1880s. John Cole is shown holding the reins on the Concord stagecoach. Richard Stetson is holding the horse in the center of the photo. (Courtesy of CAM.)

The Southern California Motor Road, operated by R.W. Button and associates, provided passenger service between Colton, San Bernardino and Riverside in the 1880s. The Colton–San Bernardino portion of the road ran along Colton Avenue. (Courtesy of CAM.)

Built in about 1887, Lincoln School was located in the center of the block between Eighth and Ninth, and D and E Streets, where the Civic Center now stands. Classes were conducted in this building until 1915, when a new building (the second Lincoln School) was built on the site. (Courtesy of CAM.)

Students and faculty of Lincoln School posed for this 1891 photograph taken at the school. The school included elementary and secondary grades until 1904, when the secondary grades moved to the new Colton High School building. (Courtesy of CAM.)

Built by Milo Gilbert in 1889, the Gilbert Building stood on the northwest corner of Eighth and I Streets. The building had a full basement and three stories above ground level, but no elevator. The ground floor housed a variety of commercial establishments. Business and professional offices occupied the second floor. The top floor was divided into furnished rooms and apartments. The building was demolished in 1934 to make way for the widening of Valley Boulevard—then known as the Ocean-to-Ocean Highway—by 20 feet to the north. (Courtesy of CAM.)

Prior to coming to Colton, Milo Gilbert had been a founder of Charles City, Iowa, where he served as the city's first mayor and built the Union Hotel, which was destroyed by fire in 1987. One of the main streets in Charles City, Gilbert Avenue, still bears his name. He settled in Colton in 1887, having already acquired property here from business deals he made while still in Charles City. He served as president of the city board of trustees from 1894 to 1897. He died in Colton in 1906 and was buried at Hermosa Cemetery. (Courtesy of CASBC.)

45

The Pacific Drug Store was located in the Gilbert Building in the early 1890s. (Courtesy of CAM.)

George Hutchinson, shown in this studio portrait, operated the Pacific Drug Store in partnership with Charles Weagant. (Courtesy of CAM.)

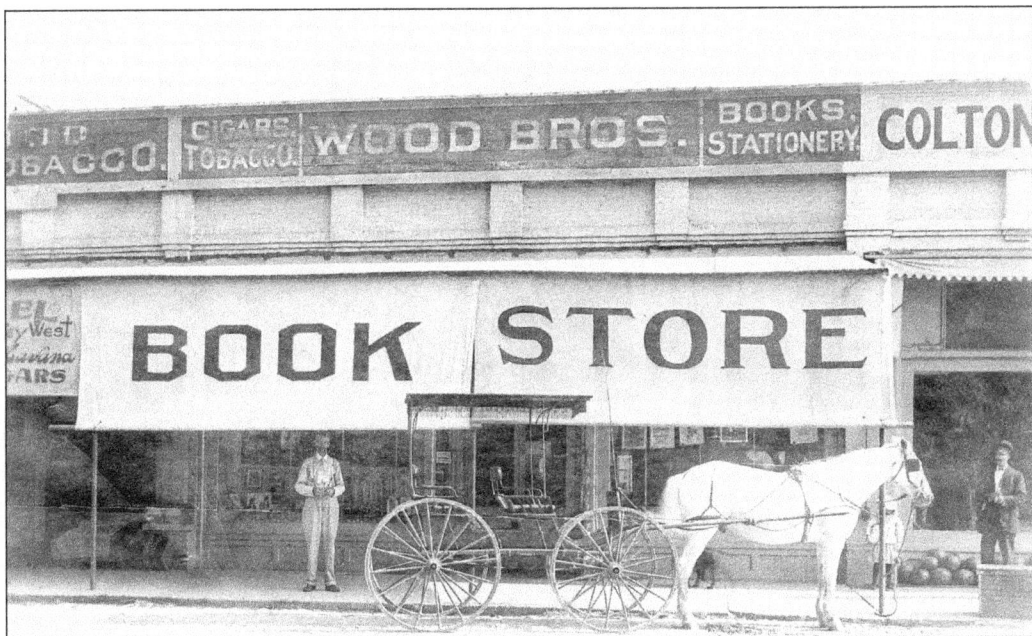

Jonas and Eugene Wood's bookstore was located on J Street between Ninth and Eighth Streets in the 1890s. (Courtesy of CAM.)

Cottage Home was a restaurant on Ninth Street near I Street in the 1890s. (Courtesy of CAM.)

The Union Block, built by Samuel Fox and his brother Dr. William Riley Fox from 1889 to 1890, was located on the southwest corner of Eighth and I Streets, diagonal to the Gilbert Building. The man (center) holding the T-square with one hand and pointing upward with the other hand is Samuel Fox. Construction of the Union Block and the Gilbert Building initiated a shift of the city's commercial center from J Street to the intersection of Eighth and I Streets. The Union Building was demolished in the 1960s as part of the city's redevelopment plan. A Mobile Gasoline station now occupies the site. (Courtesy of CAM.)

Maggie Findley Wightman was the first female commercial photographer in Colton. Several of her photographs, taken in the 1880s and 1890s, have survived, adding to our visual record of early Colton. (Courtesy of CAM.)

Maggie Findley Wightman is shown here with her husband, Ed Wightman, shortly after their marriage. (Courtesy of CAM.)

Jennie Kelting, center, operated a hat shop on the east side of Ninth Street between J and I Streets in the early 1890s. Also shown are Miss Davis, left, and Miss Hammerty, right. (Photo by Maggie Findley Wightman, courtesy of CAM.)

Maggie Findley Wightman captured this view of Colton in 1891, from a veranda on the Marlborough Hotel at Ninth and L Streets. The view is to the northwest. Note the Southern Pacific depot on the right and the commercial establishments along J Street, immediately north of the depot. (Courtesy of CAM.)

The Pioneer Lumber Company and Planing Mill, shown in this 1891 photograph taken by Maggie Findley Wightman from the Marlborough Hotel, was located on the southeast corner of K and Ninth Streets. (Courtesy of CAM.)

Built in the 1890s, this elegant Victorian house stood on the southwest corner of Ninth and L Streets. Michael A. Murphy, president of the Pioneer Lumber Company and Planing Mill, had the house built as a home for his family. He later sold it to Isaac Morris. (Courtesy of CAM.)

51

After sitting vacant for several years and falling into disrepair, the Murphy/Morris house was demolished in 2003. (Photo by Larry Sheffield.)

These happy campers are enjoying a few days at Colton's very own Camp Indolence near present-day Crestline. Camp Indolence was a tent camp used primarily by Colton residents seeking relief from summer heat in the mid-1890s. (Courtesy of CAM.)

The Colton Citrus Pavilion reflected the importance of the citrus industry in early Colton. Built under the leadership of Milo Gilbert in 1893, the Pavilion stood on the northeast corner of Tenth and I Streets on land donated by the Southern Pacific Railroad. The Pavilion hosted the California State Citrus Fair in 1893 and housed the Colton Fruit Exchange business office and packinghouse. Fire destroyed the building in March 1910. (Courtesy of CAM.)

Women made up a significant portion of the workforce in citrus packinghouses, as shown in this view of the Colton Fruit Exchange packinghouse inside the pavilion. (Courtesy of CAM.)

This *c.* 1895 photograph shows a work crew of men and boys at the Colton Cannery. So many children worked in citrus processing plants in Colton that the opening of public schools was sometimes delayed until after the packing season. (Courtesy of CAM.)

Crew members and city dignitaries posed at the Southern Pacific depot for this photograph of the bunting-draped engine that pulled President William McKinley's train during his visit to the area in 1898. Note the picture of President McKinley on top of the locomotive. (Courtesy of CAM.)

The Quarry City Band performed concerts in the "Opera House" on the second floor of City Hall in the late 1890s. (Courtesy of CAM.)

Three

HOMETOWN, U.S.A.
1900–1949

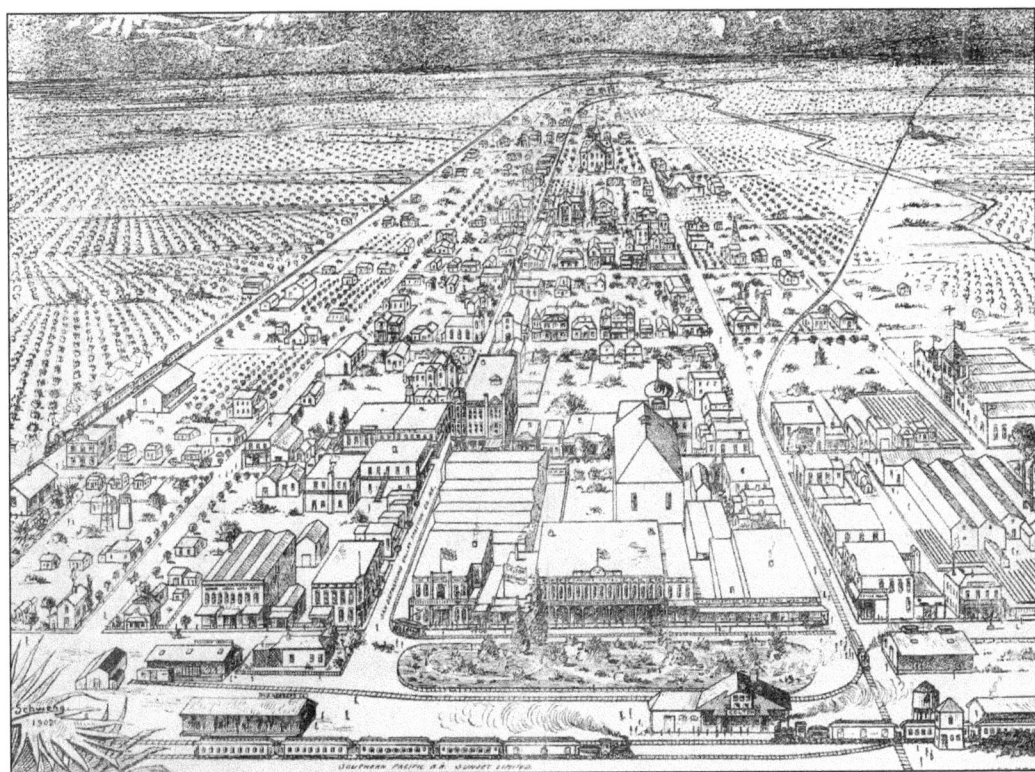

This bird's-eye view of Colton in 1902 looks to the north. The north–south streets, from left to right, are the Santa Fe Rail Road, Seventh Street, Eighth Street, Ninth Street, and Tenth Street. East–west streets, from bottom to top, are J Street, I Street, H Street, G Street, F Street, and E Street. The southern half of the city is not shown. (Courtesy of CAM.)

Ernest A. Pettijohn, a fruit grower and a director of the Colton Fruit Exchange, served as president of the city board of trustees from 1892 to 1894 and again from 1900 to 1906. (Courtesy of CAM.)

The Pettijohn family plays croquet at their home at 1136 North Eighth Street while Mrs. Pettijohn's parents stand by their automobile. Note the Pettijohn orchard to the north of the house. The house is still standing. (Courtesy of CAM.)

This early 1900s photograph shows the intersection of Ninth and I Streets. The view is along I Street to the west. (Courtesy of CAM.)

Electric trolleys powered by overhead electric cables ran on steel tracks along Eighth Street from the early 1900s until 1941, when they were replaced by motorbuses. The tracks were removed in 1942 and were used to help meet the wartime need for steel. (Courtesy of CAM.)

Colton's first firefighting equipment consisted of a hand-pulled hose cart carrying a 1,000-foot-long, two-inch hose. Two years later, the city bought a hand-drawn hook and ladder cart. The horse-drawn hose wagon shown here was purchased by the city in 1901. (Courtesy of CAM.)

In this 1902 picture of the Colton Bachelor Club are, from left to right, Doc Topriahanian, Gus Smart, Gene Howard, Fred Bruce, John Atkinson, Earl Curson, Willie Wright, and Howard Smith. Howard Smith later became a prominent banker in Colton. (Courtesy of CAM.)

Globe Mills, manufacturer of A-1 Flour, built this grain mill in Colton in 1902. The mill was located on the west side of I Street immediately west of the Santa Fe tracks. The Pillsbury Company acquired the mill in 1940 and operated it until the late 1950s, when a fire destroyed a large portion of the structure. The surviving section has been used by a variety of business since then. (Courtesy of CAM.)

Colton's first high school opened for classes in 1904. The Mission Revival building remained in use as a high school until 1923, when a new high school building was erected nearby. The old building became Roosevelt Junior High. (Courtesy of CAM.)

Built in 1906, the first Grant School was located on the southwest corner of F and Third Streets. The building remained in use as a school until 1949, when the second Grant School, located on Olive Street, opened. Slover Mountain can be seen in the background at left. (Courtesy of CAM.)

62

The Anderson Hotel, built by William M. Anderson of Idaho in 1906, was located on the southeast corner of Eighth and I Streets. The hotel originally had only two floors. Anderson had the third floor added in 1910. The Colton Redevelopment Agency closed the hotel in 1964, and the building was demolished in 1966. (Courtesy of CAM.)

The lobby of the Anderson Hotel featured columns made of marble quarried from Slover Mountain. (Courtesy of CAM.)

The dining room of the Anderson Hotel served hotel guests and was a popular meeting place for community organizations. (Courtesy of CAM.)

The dining counter in the Anderson Hotel opened in 1912. The sign on the right advertises club breakfasts for 25¢. (Courtesy of CAM.)

Colton High School's first girls' basketball team posed in their team uniforms for this 1907 photograph. (Courtesy of CAM.)

I.M. (Irvin Myers) Knopsnyder, a native of Pennsylvania, settled in Colton in 1905 and later founded Knopsnyder Mortuary, one of the most prominent businesses in Colton for nearly 70 years. (Courtesy of CAM.)

In 1907, I.M. Knopsnyder bought the St. Clair Stables, located on Seventh Street between I and J Streets, and added a horse-drawn ambulance service to the business. Later that year, he expanded the ambulance business to include undertaking and embalming services and moved the business to new quarters on the southeast corner of Seventh and I Streets. (Courtesy of CAM.)

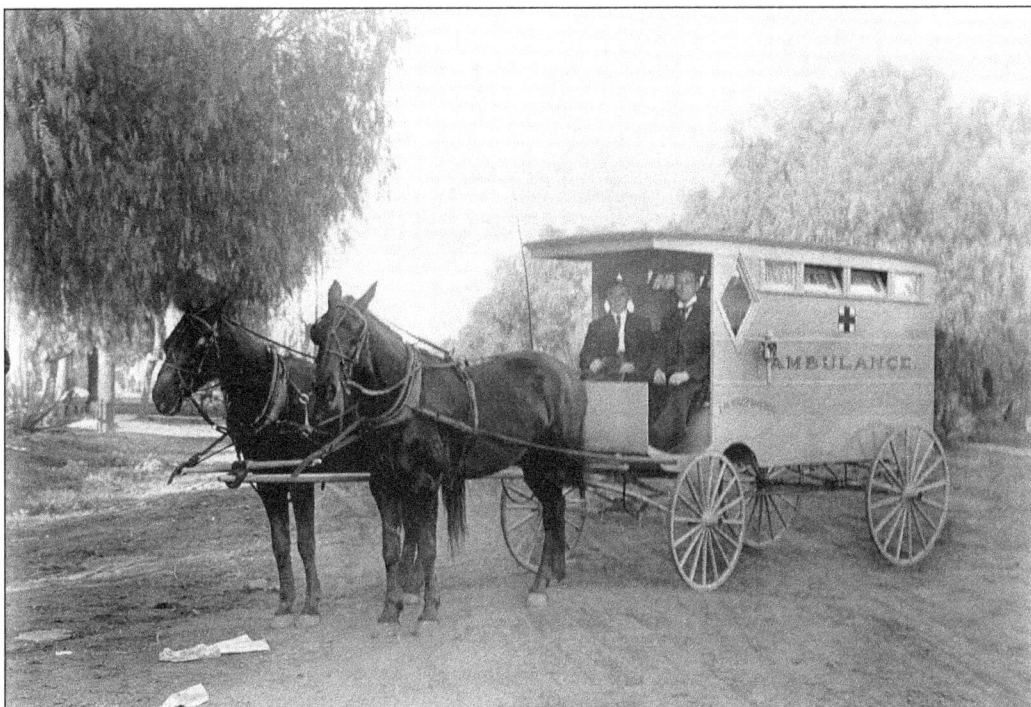

I.M. Knopsnyder, right, is shown here on his horse-drawn ambulance. The name "I.M. Knopsnyder" is printed on the ambulance above the front wheel. (Courtesy of CAM.)

Workers and passersby posed for this c. 1907 photograph of the Colton Carnegie Public Library building under construction. (Courtesy of CAM.)

E. Muschewske, a harness maker and buggy dealer, had just organized the Colton Band when this photograph was taken on the steps of the Colton Public Library in 1908. (Courtesy of CAM.)

Members of the Colton Band changed the band's name to Swinnerton's Colton Band in 1910, when they elected Jimmy Swinnerton, the famed cartoonist for Hearst newspapers, as their band manager. William Randolph Hearst, Swinnerton's boss, had sent him to Colton in 1906, believing the climate here would help him recover from tuberculosis and alcoholism. Swinnerton lived in Colton until 1914, when he moved to Flagstaff, Arizona. He died in 1974 at the age of 98 years. Also shown in the photograph are two baseball teams. (Courtesy of CAM.)

The California Portland Cement Plant began mining limestone for the manufacture of portland cement on Slover Mountain in 1892. This photograph shows the plant and mountain in 1909. Note the dust from blasting. The mountain is named after Isaac Slover, a hunter and former Rocky Mountain trapper, who lived at the base of the mountain with his New Mexican wife, Barbara, from the early 1840s until 1854, when he was killed by a grizzly bear. (Courtesy of CAM.)

Colton's volunteer firefighters posed with their horse-drawn fire wagon in front of the fire station in City Hall on I Street for this 1910 photograph. (Courtesy of CAM.)

Automobiles would soon replace horse-drawn wagons on Colton's downtown streets. This view, taken c. 1910, shows the intersection of Eighth and I Streets looking east on I Street. The building on the left, rising slightly above the tree, is Society Hall. The turreted building east of Society Hall is the Gilbert Building. The onion-domed building on the right is City Hall. Directly west of City Hall is the Anderson Hotel. The building west of the Anderson is the Union Block. (Courtesy of CAM.)

Garfield School, located on the northwest corner of Eighth and N Streets, was built in 1910 and remained in use as an elementary school until 1928, when it was destroyed by fire. The Sombrero Market now stands on the site. (Courtesy of CAM.)

Young Coltonites enjoy an outing in a citrus grove, c. 1910. (Courtesy of CAM.)

Nellie Cocking modeled a fashionable dress for this c. 1910 photograph. Note the mirror image showing the back of the dress. (Courtesy of CAM.)

Robert Johnston Martin, a fruit grower, served as the twelfth president of the city board of trustees (1908–1911.) He and two of his fellow trustees were recalled from office in the city's first recall election (1911) because they supported denial of a permit to open a saloon in the Anderson Hotel. (Courtesy of CAM.)

Evert Hines is making his rounds for the San Bernardino Valley Gas Company. (Courtesy of Don Hines.)

Members of the Colton Motor Cycle Club displayed their machines for this 1912 photograph taken at the Union Block on I Street. (Courtesy of CAM.)

The Jewell Memorial Methodist Episcopal Church stood on the northwest corner of Eighth and H Streets until it was destroyed by fire in 1912. Following the fire, the congregation held its services in the basement of the Colton Carnegie Public Library while a new chapel was under construction. (Courtesy of CAM.)

Born in England in 1848, the Reverend Isaac Jewell immigrated to the United States in his youth and prepared for the ministry at Yale University. He joined the Southern California Methodist Conference in 1894 and was pastor of the Colton Methodist Episcopal Church at the time of his death in 1908. The Colton congregation changed its name to the Jewell Memorial Methodist Episcopal Church in his honor in 1910. (Courtesy of CAM.)

When fire destroyed the Jewell Memorial Methodist Church building in 1912, the congregation built this meetinghouse on the northeast corner of Eighth and G Streets. The congregation continued to hold services in the building until 1959, when it moved to a new church building on Laurel Street. The G Street building was demolished in 1964. The site is now occupied by a gas station and convenience store. (Courtesy of CAM.)

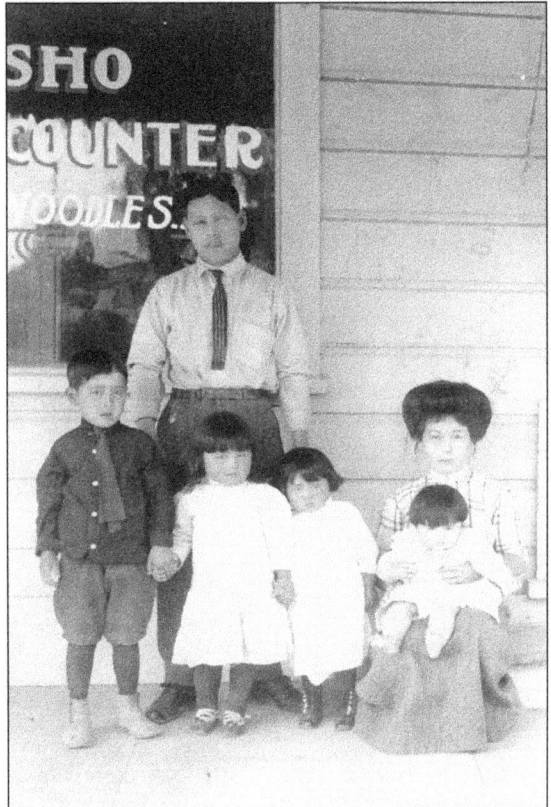

Mr. and Mrs. Oye, shown here with their children, operated a restaurant and lunch counter on J Street around 1913. (Courtesy of CAM.)

The city purchased this Seagrave Pumper in 1914. The engine was one of only two delivered to Southern California that year. Being the only pumper in the San Bernardino Valley at the time, the engine was occasionally sent to fight fires in San Bernardino and Redlands. (Courtesy of CAM.)

Pictured in this 1914 photograph are members of the Colton Fire Department with their new Seagrave Pumper, in front of the fire station in city hall. (Courtesy of CAM.)

Nearly everyone in town turned out for the Pioneer Day parade held as part of the weeklong Colton Carnival in October 1914. The political campaign banner urged voters to cast their ballots for Ray Riley and W.J. Kincaid for county supervisors. Riley was a Colton man who owned the drug store shown near the right edge of the photograph. Both men won. Note the El Camino Real bell near the utility pole on the left. The bell has since disappeared. The setting of the photograph is Eighth Street near I Street, looking northeast. (Courtesy of CAM.)

Civil War veterans and guests posed for this photograph of their Grand Army of the Republic float, which rode in the Colton Carnival Week Pioneer Day parade in October 1914. (Courtesy of CAM.)

Trudy Zempleburg (holding the steering wheel), queen of Colton Carnival Week, and her court grace the fire department's new Seagrave Pumper in front of City Hall. Trudy later moved to San Francisco, where she worked for the Swiss Consulate. (Courtesy of CAM.)

Giovanni Console, right, promoted the healing power of mineral water from springs on his homestead in Reche Canyon at this booth during Colton Carnival Week, 1914. Console claimed his water cured a multitude of ailments, including infertility. "There's a baby in every five gallons," he said with a smile, " and I gotta sixteen kids to prove it." (Courtesy of CAM.)

The second Lincoln School was built in 1915 and remained in use as a school until 1956, when it was demolished to make way for the Civic Center, which now occupies the site. (Courtesy of CAM.)

Pictured here is a classroom of students at Lincoln School in 1916. (Courtesy of CAM.)

By the time this photograph was taken, automobiles had replaced horse-drawn wagons on downtown streets. The view is toward the east along I Street from Seventh Street. The turreted building on the left is the Gilbert Building. (Courtesy of CAM.)

Friend Lombra (right) introduced the first motorized truck into Colton, thus initiating a new era in freight hauling. Lombra later served as chief of the Colton Fire Department. (Courtesy of CAM.)

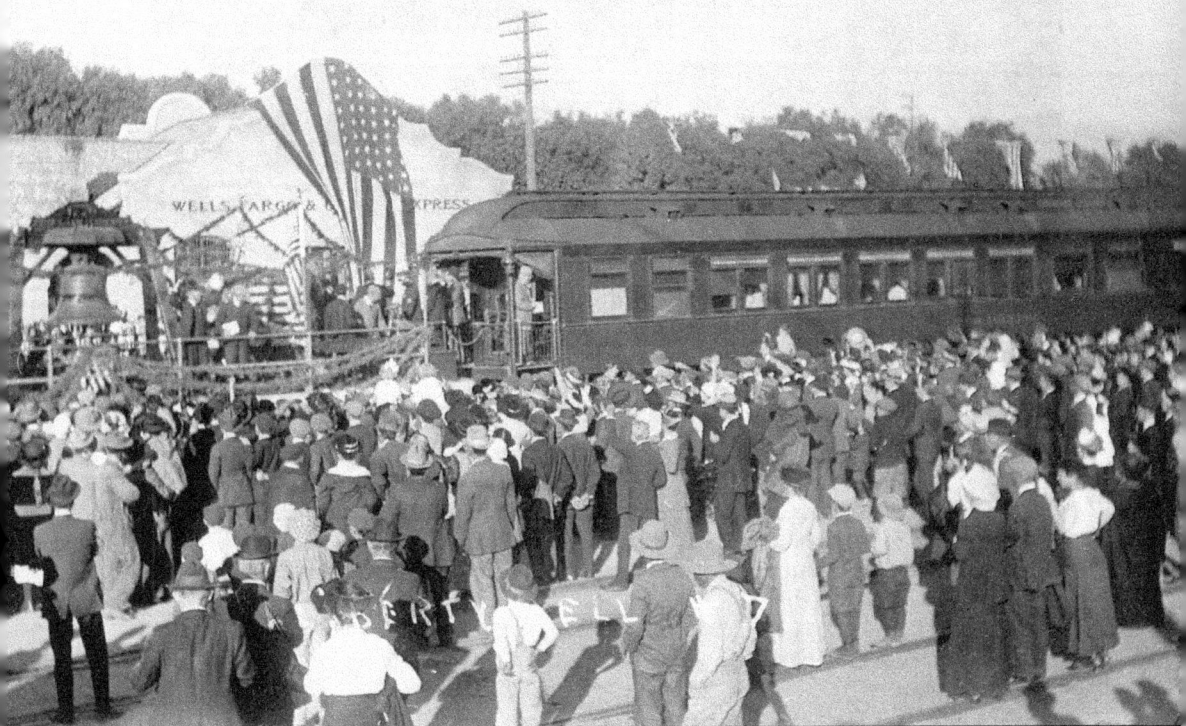

Hundreds of people from neighboring cities came to Colton in November 1915 to see the Liberty Bell when it made a 28-minute stop at the Southern Pacific depot. The stop in Colton was part of a cross-country tour as the bell was transported home to Philadelphia from New Orleans, where it had been on display at the World Exhibition. (Courtesy of CAM.)

Women of the Colton American Red Cross Canteen contributed to the World War I war effort by serving refreshments to service men in transit at the Southern Pacific depot. (Courtesy of CAM.)

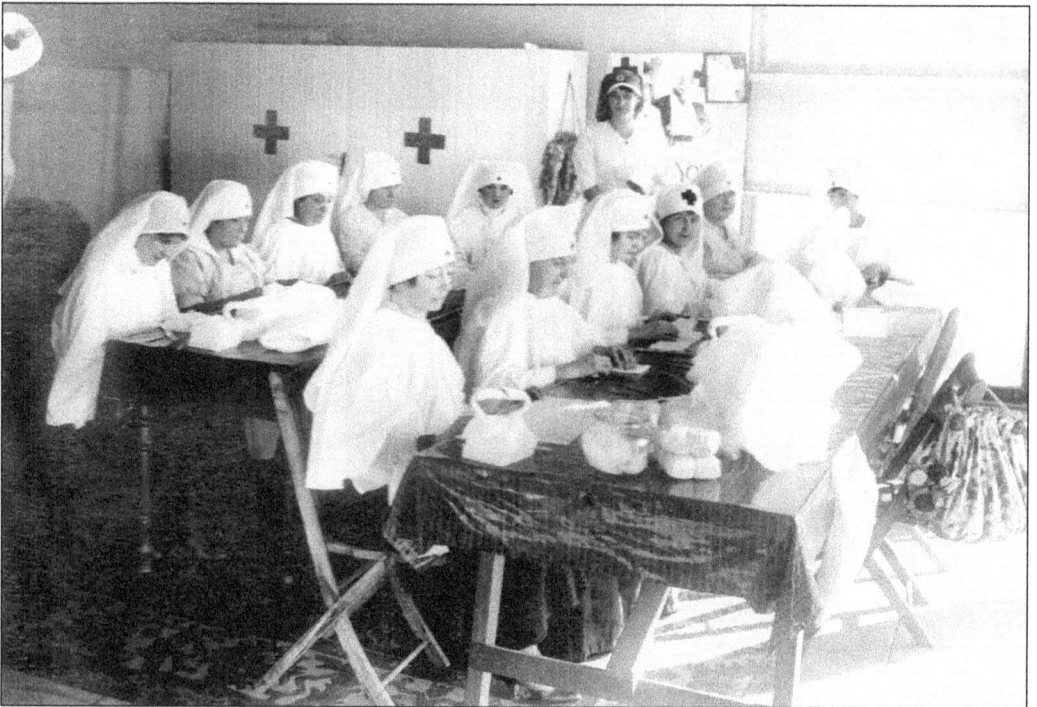
Colton Red Cross volunteers are shown here assembling bandages during World War I. (Courtesy of CAM.)

The Colton Plunge, built in 1921 in the Municipal Park, now Cesar Chavez Park, was billed as the largest open-air swimming pool in California. The unheated pool was supplied with warm water by a well donated to the city by Ormiston L. Emery. People came from as far away as 100 miles to enjoy the refreshing water. (Courtesy of CAM.)

Jack Marks, shown in this 1922 photograph, was Colton's first motorcycle cop. It was said his motorcycle could reach a speed of 90 miles per hour. (Courtesy of CAM.)

From 1930 through the 1960s, South Seventh Street, between K and N Streets, was a lively commercial district and the heart of South Colton's Latino community. Latino markets, dry goods stores, restaurants, tortilla makers, pool rooms, and dance halls, interspersed with the San Salvador Church and family homes, lined the sides of the street. It was the place to shop and to gather with friends. Today, the Seventh Street Market is one of only two businesses still in operation on the street. The other is the El Sombrero nightclub. (Photo by Larry Sheffield.)

Pictured here are Jesus Morales, left, owner of the Seventh Street Market, and Bobby Vasquez, a historian of South Colton. (Photo by Larry Sheffield.)

The Vasquez family was among the many Latino families who settled in South Colton during or shortly after the Mexican Revolution of 1910. Gonzalo Vasquez (left) and Marina Vasquez (right) were born in Guanajuto, Mexico, where they met and married. When the Mexican Revolution of 1910 broke out following the collapse of the Diaz regime, Gonzalo Vasquez joined the Federal Army, but later switched to the army of Pancho Villa. Marina Vasquez accompanied her husband in Villa's army as a *soldadera*, one of the many women who served as spouses, soldiers, and maids, in revolutionary-era Mexican armies. The young couple crossed into the United States at El Paso in 1915 and moved in 1921 to South Colton, where they joined Marina's brother, Esso Lopez, and other relatives who had already settled there. Also shown are Gonzalo's brother, David Vasquez, sitting on chair, and Gonzalo and Marina's two children, Mary (left) and Norberto (sitting on David's lap). (Courtesy of Bobby Vasquez.)

The First Baptist Church of Colton began holding services in its new church building in 1927. The church is located at 170 West F Street. (Courtesy of CAM.)

The remodeled city hall on I Street, just east of the Anderson Hotel, provides the background for this *c.* 1927 photograph of firefighters and their engines. (Courtesy of CAM.)

Colton firefighters built this clubhouse in 1927. The clubhouse was located near Big Bear Lake. (Courtesy of CAM.)

Roosevelt Junior High School opened for classes in this building in 1928. The school was located on the north side of I Street between Second and Third Streets, now a part of the campus of Colton High School. Roosevelt Jr. High moved to Colton Middle School on Laurel Street and Valencia Drive in 1954. (Courtesy of CAM.)

Dozens of children attended the annual 1929 Christmas party held by Jose and Refugio Aguilera, at their La Nueva Reforma Groceries and Dry Goods store. The store was located at 356 West N Street in South Colton and remained in business until the late 1940s. (Courtesy of CAM.)

Shown here, from left to right, are Refugio Aguilera, an unidentified employee, and Effie Aguileria (partially visible), at work in La Nueva Reforma Groceries and Dry Goods store. (Courtesy of CAM.)

The new Colton High School opened for classes in 1923. (Courtesy of CAM.)

Men of the Colton American Legion Post 155 are on their way home from the American Legion National Convention held in San Francisco, October 15–19, 1923. The photograph was taken on October 24, 1923, in Los Angeles. (Courtesy of CAM.)

The second Garfield School was built in 1927. The school was located on Eighth Street, just south of the present-day Woodrow Wilson School. (Courtesy of California State University San Bernardino.)

The Colton Police Department is shown in 1927. (Courtesy of CAM.)

The children shown in this 1927 photograph, taken at the San Salvador Church in South Colton, have just received their first communion. Father A. Barrios is standing at the top center. (Courtesy of California State University San Bernardino.)

Members of the Colton Fortnightly Club gathered at the Anderson Hotel in 1928 to honor Mrs. Wilkerson on her birthday. Pictured in front is Mrs. Wilkerson (honoree); and, from left to right, (sitting) Mrs. Ethel Bailey, Mrs. Billie Witmer, Mrs. Viola Jantzen Pritchard, Mrs. Helen Smith, Mrs. Myrtle Knopsnyder, and Mrs. Sadie Butterfield; (standing) Mrs. M.O. Hert, Mrs. Jess Bartlett, Mrs. Samuel Andrews, Mrs. Sumner Wright, and Mrs. Genevieve Smith. (Courtesy of CAM.)

Built for the chamber of commerce in 1928, this building served as the chamber's home until 1954, when it was demolished to make way for Interstate 10. The building was located at the southeast corner of Eighth and J Streets, on a section of the Southern Pacific Railroad Park. The chamber of commerce moved to new quarters on H Street. (Courtesy of the Colton Chamber of Commerce.)

Three young men examine an airplane at the Colton Airport, c. 1928. The airport was located on the northwest corner of Mt. Vernon and Colton Avenues. (Courtesy of CAM.)

I.M. Knopsnyder had this two-story Mission Revival–style building erected on the northeast corner of Seventh and G Streets in 1930 to 1931 as the new home for his mortuary. The mortuary continued to be operated as a family business until 1972, when the family leased it to Bob Heinz of Bloomington's Green Acres, Inc. The mortuary business has since been discontinued, and the building is now for sale as commercial space. (Courtesy of CAM.)

The Depression-era Public Works Administration (PWA) built this post office in 1935. The post office was located on Eighth Street, between the present-day Bank of America and the alley. It remained in use until 1970, when the current post office on Seventh Street opened. (Courtesy of CAM.)

The Work Projects Administration (WPA) built this Spanish Revival–style fire station in 1935. The station is located on the northeast corner of Tenth and E Streets and is still in use. (Courtesy of CAM.)

WPA Federal Theater productions were popular events in Colton. *Enter Madam*, advertised in this poster, was one of several Federal Theater road shows that came to Colton in the 1930s. The project was disbanded in 1939 under pressure from conservative critics of the New Deal, who claimed the performances promoted New Deal propaganda. A few present-day Colton residents remember having attended these popular shows. (Courtesy of CAM.)

FEDERAL THEATRE
LA CADENA AND MT. VERNON
Enter Madam
JUNE 9-12
PRICES 10¢ 20¢ 30¢
DIV. W.P.A.

Federal Theater road shows were often staged in tents. The tent shown in this *c.* 1935 photograph was located at La Cadena Drive and Mt. Vernon Avenue. The photograph is by Dorothea Lange, famed Depression-era photographer. (Courtesy of CAM.)

The Squall, advertised in this WPA Federal Theater poster, was staged in South Colton. (Courtesy of CAM.)

Surging water during the flood of 1938 undermined the supports for these railroad tracks near the Southern Pacific yard. (Courtesy of CAM.)

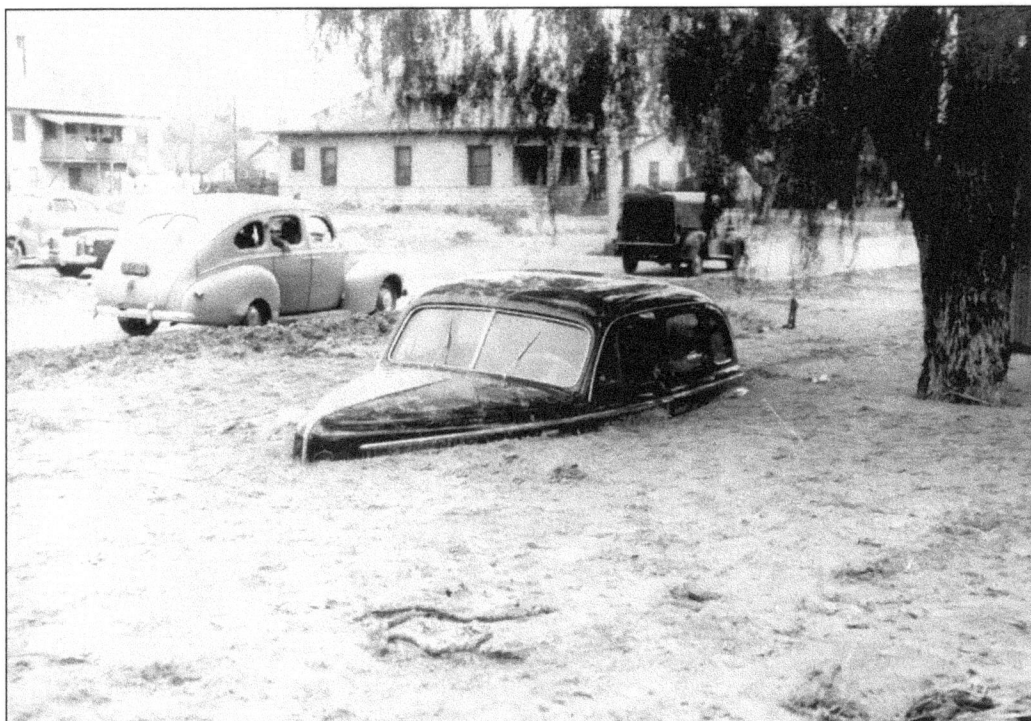

The flood of 1938 left this new car mired in mud. (Courtesy of CAM.)

This view of the Southern Pacific roundhouse shows the turntable used for switching engines. (Courtesy of CAM.)

The *Sunset Limited* is shown here pulling into the Colton station. The *Sunset Limited* was named after the Southern Pacific Railroad's Sunset Route, which extended from Los Angeles to New Orleans, a distance of slightly more than 2,000 miles. (Courtesy of CAM.)

Approximately 2,000 Colton men and women served in the armed forces during World War II. Shown in this 1943 photograph taken in front of the public library is a Roll of Honor identifying Colton residents who were serving in the armed forces at the time. (Courtesy of CAM.)

This undated photograph, taken sometime during the post–World War II years, records an important event in the history of ethnic relations in Colton. After the war, in which some 300 Latino men and women had served in the armed forces, leaders from South and North Colton sought ways to unify the two communities, which had traditionally been segregated into Latino South Colton and Anglo North Colton. The photo shows Latino and Anglo business and community leaders meeting for a chamber of commerce–sponsored dinner at the American Legion Post 155, in a fledgling effort to unify the two communities. The sole woman in the photograph is Hazel Freeman, secretary of the chamber of commerce. (Courtesy of the Colton Chamber of Commerce.)

John Martinez Perez, at right, with Ralph Binford, center, and Manuel Ortiz, left, was the first Latino to serve on the Colton City Council. Guided in his political development by Pete S. Luque Sr., Perez won election to City Council in 1948 and served until 1951, when he resigned. At his recommendation, the council appointed Pete S. Luque Sr., as his successor. (Courtesy of Joe Perez.)

Prior to his election to the Colton City Council, John Martinez Perez (left) fought as a welterweight contender under the name of Johnnie Martinez. He is shown here as the trainer of Savas Robledo, a Colton boxer. (Courtesy of Joe Perez.)

Cliff Ham's full-service Hub City Service Center was located on the northwest corner of Eighth and H Streets. Ham served on City Council from 1948 to 1950 and was postmaster from 1949 to 1956. (Courtesy of CAM.)

This snapshot of the September 16, 1947 Mexican Independence Day car-parade headed south along Eighth Street, toward I Street, gives a view of mid-century downtown Colton. The theatre on the right is the Hub City Theatre. (Courtesy of Joe Lucero, Joe Nunez, Rudy Oliva, Frank Sanchez, Rodolfo [Rudy] Serrano, and Bobby Vasquez.)

The Arcade, shown here behind the car decorated with a Mexican flag for the Fiesta Day parade on September 16, 1947, featured a Mode O' Day dress shop and the Arcade Drugstore and soda fountain. The second floor housed offices. The Arcade was razed in 1966 as part of a downtown redevelopment project. (Courtesy of Joe Lucero, Joe Nunez, Rudy Oliva, Frank Sanchez, Rodolfo [Rudy] Sanchez, and Bobby Vasquez.)

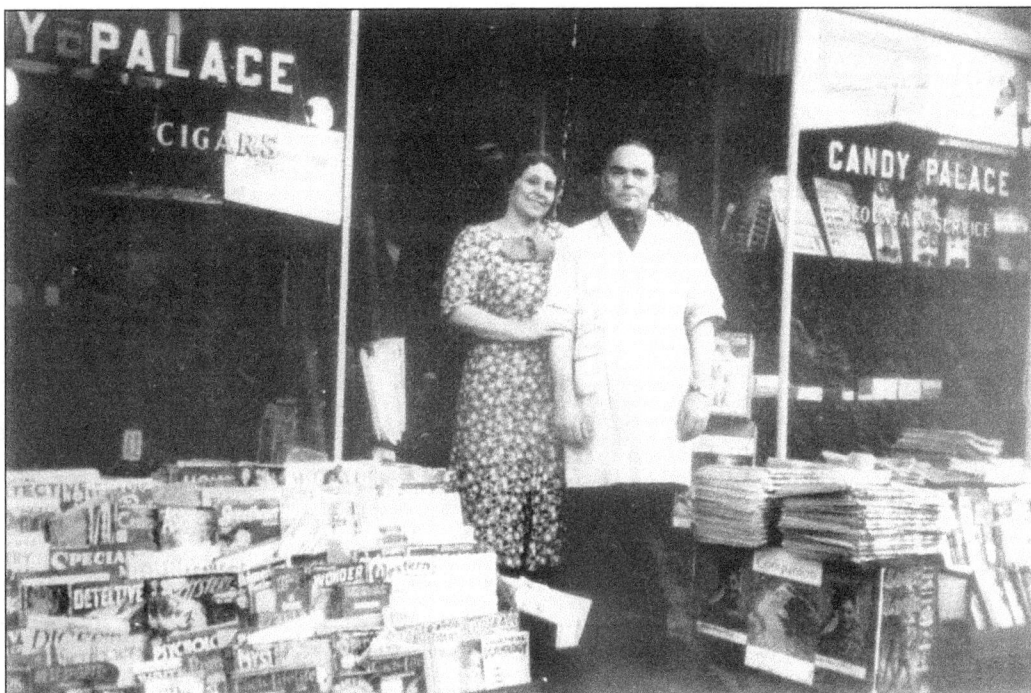

Thaddeus and Mattie Montgomery were the owners of the Candy Palace, a popular confectionery and soda fountain located at 276 North Eighth Street, next door to the Arcade. (Courtesy of CAM.)

The soda fountain in the Candy Palace was a good place to meet with friends and enjoy a refreshment. (Courtesy of CAM.)

Pictured is downtown Colton around 1949, looking south on Eighth Street from I Street. (Courtesy of CAM.)

Here is another view of downtown Colton, looking north on Eighth Street. (Courtesy of CAM.)

Four

SUBURBAN COMMUNITY 1950–PRESENT

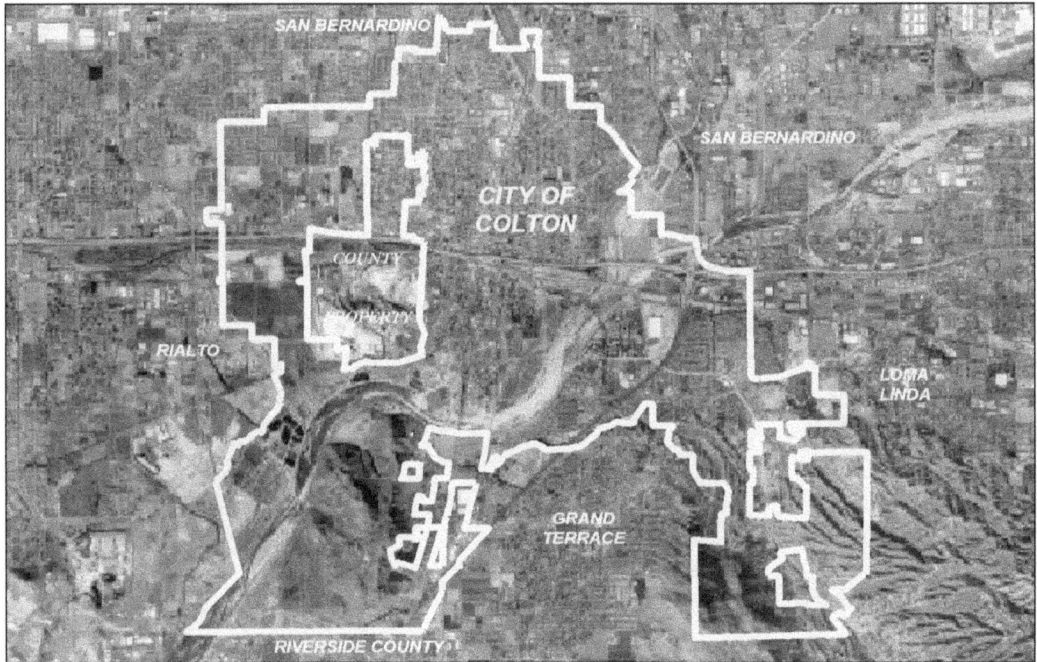

Pictured are the boundaries of present-day Colton. The city comprises an area of nearly 18 square miles and has an estimated population of 50,572 people. (Image by Philip Hinojos, GIS Technician, City of Colton.)

Remnants of Colton's first commercial district are shown here just before their demolition in 1953 to make way for Interstate 10. John W. Davis Sr. erected the two-story brick building in 1886 to house his newly formed First National Bank of Colton. The first meeting of the Colton City Board of Trustees, now called City Council, met in this building in 1887. In later years, the second floor provided apartments for newcomers to Colton while they searched for permanent housing. By the time this photo was taken, Helman's Department Store had moved to Eighth and H Streets, where it remained until 1968, when it moved to the northwest corner of Eighth and I Streets. (Courtesy of the Colton Chamber of Commerce.)

Pictured here is Interstate 10 under construction. Note the Eighth Street on-ramp. (Courtesy of the Colton Chamber of Commerce.)

Dolores Valdez (center), the queen of the 1957 Mexican Independence Day festival, commands her court. (Courtesy of California State University San Bernardino.)

This building on the southeast corner of La Cadena Drive (formerly Eighth Street) and E Street was Craigmiles's Fountain, also known as "Hogan's Hangout" in the 1940s. The Thorpes bought the business from Craigmiles in 1947 and converted it into Jim Thorpe's Restaurant. Jean and Gigi Irola bought the restaurant in 1964 and turned it into Jean's French Restaurant, which now occupies the site. (Courtesy of the Colton Chamber of Commerce.)

When the chamber of commerce building on J Street was demolished in 1954 to make way of Interstate 10, the chamber moved to new quarters, shown here, at 171 East H Street. (Courtesy of the Colton Chamber of Commerce.)

Colton Middle School, on the corner of Laurel Street and Valencia Drive, opened for classes in 1954. The school combined Roosevelt Junior High and Woodrow Wilson Junior High. (Courtesy of CAM.)

Four former mayors and the incumbent posed for this photograph taken at the Colton Homecoming in June 1955. Pictured, from left to right, are Samuel E. Andrews (1926–1928), Eugene McKersie (1945–1946), Charles C. Watson (1950–1952), Paul Young (1952–1954), and Alva Duke, the incumbent. (Courtesy of CAM.)

Colton mayor Woodrow Miller (left) greets Adlai Stevenson (right) during Stevenson's campaign for the presidency in 1956. Also shown is Mellvine Fuchs. (Courtesy of the Colton Chamber of Commerce.)

When the City of Colton adopted the council-manager form of city government in 1956, the Colton City Council hired Lyman Cozad as the first city manager. Cozad held the job until 1964, when he resigned to become the administrative officer of the city of Beverly Hills. (Courtesy of CAM.)

Members of the Colton City Council posed for this c. 1959 photograph. Pictured, from left to right, are Martin Matich (mayor), John M. "Mac" Coltrin, Woodrow Miller, Clinton Smith, and Mellvine Fuchs. Woodrow Miller had already served as mayor from 1956 to 1958. Mellvine Fuchs served as mayor from 1960 to 1962, and Mac Coltrin served as mayor from 1964 to 1966. (Courtesy of CAM.)

Pictured is the intersection of La Cadena Drive and Valley Boulevard (formerly I Street) around 1960. (Courtesy of CAM.)

Woodrow Miller, president of the Miller Honey Company, draws a winning ticket from a baseball cap held by Carl T. Rimbaugh as Perry Winsted looks on at the baseball field at Colton Municipal Park, 1960. Carl Rimbaugh, a founder of the Colton Girls Little League, was director of the Western States Little League at the time of the photograph. Perry Winstead was a founder of the California Little League. (Courtesy of the Colton Chamber of Commerce.)

Retiring chamber of commerce president Don McIntosh (center) passes the gavel to president-elect R. Glen De Yoe, at a meeting of the chamber of commerce board of directors, 1961. Also shown, from left to right, are (sitting) Paul Rogers, Paul Snively, Ray Hunter, and Bill Potthoff; (standing) John Kok, Ward Hughes (vice president-elect), and Harold Winters. (Courtesy of the Colton Chamber of Commerce.)

The Colton Civic Center at 650 North La Cadena Drive was dedicated on February 11, 1961. Building architect Herman O. Ruhnau said the city's informal name of "Hub City" inspired the center's circular design. (Courtesy of the Colton Chamber of Commerce.)

This photo shows a meeting of the Colton City Council in the new Civic Center, c. 1961. Pictured, from left to right, are John M. "Mac" Coltrin (council member), Elizabeth Davis (city clerk), Lawrence A. Hutton (city attorney), Melvine Fuchs (mayor), Lyman Cozad (city manager), Carl T. Rimbaugh (council member), and Pasqual Oliva (council member). (Courtesy of CAM.)

Pasqual Oliva served as mayor of Colton from 1966 to 1968. (Courtesy of the Colton Chamber of Commerce.)

L.C. Myers's New Colton Theater was located at 250 East I Street until 1967, when it was demolished as part of a downtown redevelopment project. (Courtesy of CAM.)

This aerial view shows downtown Colton in the early 1970s after various redevelopment projects had replaced most of the older buildings with new structures. The street running parallel to the freeway is Valley Boulevard. Note Stater Brothers Market just to left of the empty field. (Courtesy of the Colton Chamber of Commerce.)

Colton mayor Abe Beltran (left) shared a grip of solidarity with Cesar Chavez for this c. 1972 photograph taken in Colton. Beltran worked with Chavez in organizing the United Farm Workers in the 1960s. Also shown, from left to right, are Joa Beltran, Teresa Beltran, Marta Macias, and an unknown woman. (Courtesy of Abe Beltran.)

116

Ranked among the top two percent of high school marching bands in the United States, the Colton High School Marching Band attended the invitational Geneva Festival held in Lucerne, Switzerland, in 1973. The band is shown here marching in a parade in downtown Colton in 1974. (Courtesy of the Colton Chamber of Commerce.)

Albert Huntoon was Colton's first publicly elected mayor. Prior to his election in 1974, City Council members chose one of their own to serve as mayor. (Courtesy of Pauline Huntoon.)

117

The Colton Rotary Club, shown in this 1974 photograph, has been part of the city's social scene since 1922. (Courtesy of the Colton Chamber of Commerce.)

The Lawrence A. Hutton Community Center on Colton Avenue opened in 1978. The facility is now a senior center. (Photo by Larry Sheffield.)

The sign at left, a familiar landmark along Interstate 10, was taken down in the late 1980s. Colton has been known as "the hub" since 1877, when the name began appearing in a local newspaper. (Courtesy of the Colton Chamber of Commerce.)

Pictured here are the Little Miss Colton contestants for 1987. Miss Colton, Jodi Cochran (right), holds the winner, Vanessa Miranda. (Courtesy of the Colton Chamber of Commerce.)

Located just east of the Hutton Senior Center, this community center opened in 1995. The center features a basketball gymnasium, an exercise room, and community meeting rooms. It also houses the offices of the city Parks and Recreation Department. City Council named the facility the Frank A. Gonzales Community Center in 2003. (Photo by Larry Sheffield.)

This building in Cesar Chavez Park has served the community in a variety of ways. Built as a Boy Scout cabin in 1927, it was used as a little theater in the 1960s and is now the Savas Robledo Boxing Gymnasium. (Photo by Larry Sheffield.)

La Cadena Drive is known for the architectural diversity of its homes. The long sloping rear roof on the Tucci home, located at 1145 North La Cadena Drive, formerly Eighth Street, gives it its New England Saltbox architectural style. It is the only Saltbox-style home in Colton and one of only a few in the state. (Photo by Larry Sheffield, courtesy of Ron and Ane Tucci.)

This Craftsman-style house features stone work composed of stones quarried from Slover Mountain. The house is now the office of architect Jon Zane. (Photo by Larry Sheffield, courtesy of Jon Zane.)

The Ashley House is a good example of Queen Anne architecture. Built in the 1880s, the house was originally located on the north side of F Street between Eighth and Ninth Streets and was moved to its present location at 736 North La Cadena Drive in 1951. The house is named after Bill and Betty Ashley, who owned it from 1968 to 1988. (Courtesy of CAM.)

The Ashley House is shown here at its original location on F Street between Eighth and Ninth Streets. (Courtesy of CAM.)

Built in the 1880s, this Eastlake Queen Anne Victorian, known as the Hanna House, was originally located at 141 East F Street. The Wilson Hanna family bought the house in 1923 and had it moved to its present location at 712 North La Cadena Drive in 1951, when a Safeway market was slated for construction on the F Street site. (Courtesy of CAM.)

Wilson C. Hanna, longtime occupant of the Hanna House, displays a marble pen holder presented to him by his associates at the California Portland Cement Company in recognition of his 60 years of distinguished employment with the company. An avid collector of bird eggs, Hanna created a collection of over 200,000 bird eggs from around the world and achieved national recognition as an oologist. His collection of bird eggs is now on display at the San Bernardino County. (Courtesy of CAM.)

124

Mayor Frank A. Gonzales cuts the ribbon for the grand opening of the Colton Area Museum, December 1991. Pictured, from left to right, are David Zamora, Jon Zane, Frances Galloway, Evelyn Rehrer, Hazel E. Olson (president), Pauline Huntoon (vice president), Jo Soares (treasurer), unidentified, Donald Hines, Richard Dawson, Margaret Matich, Raymond Hunter, and Paula Olson (secretary). (Courtesy of CAM.)

The Arrowhead Regional Medical Center, formerly the San Bernardino County Medical Center, has been located in Colton since the early 1990s. (Photo by Larry Sheffield.)

Colton firefighters placed this statue in front of the Colton Fire Station No. 1 in 2003 to honor the bravery of firefighters during the terrorist attacks in New York City on September 11, 2001. Al's Garden Art donated the statue. (Photo by Larry Sheffield.)

Pictured are members of the Colton High School Class of 1945 at a mini-reunion, held at the Sizzler Restaurant in Fontana, March 2004. Pictured, from left to right, are (front row) Dorothy Hert Noriega, Les Brower, Mary Matus Alanis, Betty Brown Vargas, Jennie Esquer Rubio, Juana Sanchez Adame, Rita Sanchez Gonzales, Sally Reyman Brin, Marie Ligon Pound, Andre Tomatis, Bill Macias, and Bob Alvarez; (back row) June May Beal, John Cherry, Stella Sharp (widow of Bill Sharp), Jay East, Jesse Nunez, Delbert Crane, Elaine May Tully, Dorothy Kinsey Castle, Shirley Miller Jones, Kermit Hayden, Charles Pine, and Adrian Enderson. (Courtesy of Bob Alvarez.)

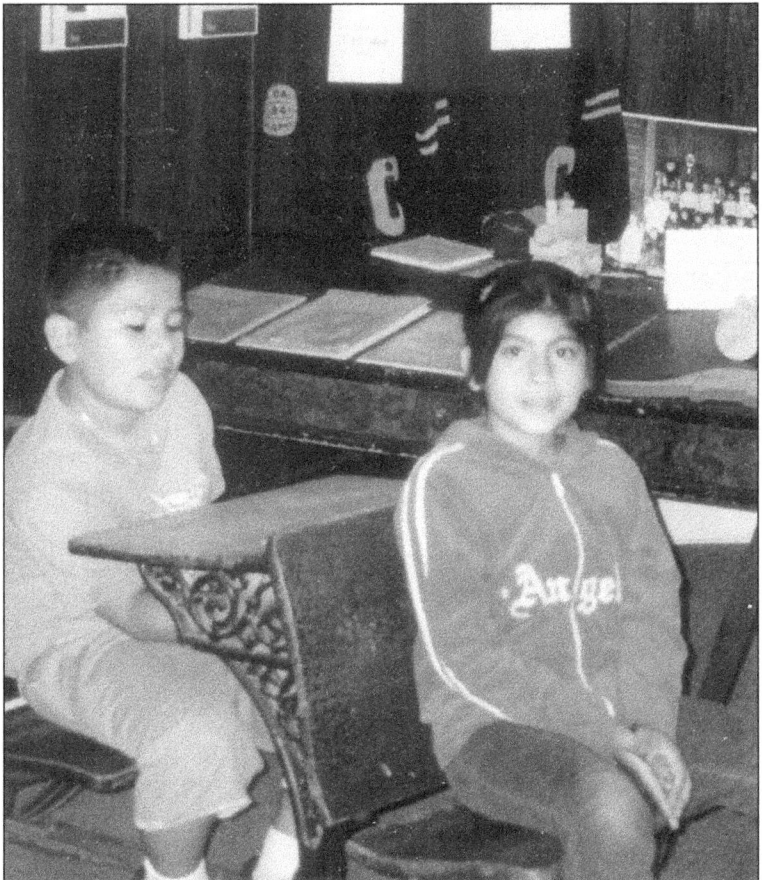

Jorge Rivera tries out an old-fashioned school desk during a visit to the Colton Area Museum with his second grade class from Alice Birney School in April 2004. Also shown is his classmate, Elizabeth Banuelos. (Photo by Larry Sheffield.)

Colton Dry Cleaners has been doing business in downtown Colton for 109 years. Max Zempleburg initiated the business in 1895, when he began providing a pressing and cleaning service in his men's clothing store on Eighth and J Streets. The business has since had several owners, including Alva Duke, a former mayor, and has changed locations several times. It is currently located on the southeast corner of La Cadena Drive and H Street, and is owned and operated by John and Young Kim. (Photo by Larry Sheffield.)

www.ingramcontent.com/pod-product-compliance
Lightning Source LLC
Chambersburg PA
CBHW080614110426
42813CB00006B/1506